The
SWANS
go up!

The SWANS go up!

Geraint H. Jenkins

y Lolfa

I'm hwyrion
Maïwenn Enfys, Dafydd Euros a Myfanwy Hannah,
Jacs y dyfodol

To my grandchildren
Maïwenn Enfys, Dafydd Euros and Myfanwy Hannah,
Jacks of the future

First impression: 2011
© Geraint H. Jenkins & Y Lolfa Cyf., 2011

Photographs: Huw Evans Agency & Chris Reynolds
Photo of Roberto Martinez by Darryl Corner
Cover design: Y Lolfa

ISBN: 978 184771 404 6

Printed on acid-free and partly recycled paper
and published and bound in Wales by
Y Lolfa Cyf., Talybont, Ceredigion SY24 5HE
e-mail ylolfa@ylolfa.com
website www.ylolfa.com
tel 01970 832 304
fax 832 782

Contents

Foreword

L AST SEASON'S PROMOTION-WINNING campaign was
the most thrilling high point of my career.
This must-read book tells the story of the
Swans' rise to the Premiership in a vivid way.
It will bring back wonderful memories for the
Jack Army.

Garry Monk

Preface

THIS BOOK HAS been a labour of love. I've been a fervent supporter of Swansea City Football Club since 1964 when, as a callow university fresher and budding Welsh historian, I joined the Jacks on the terraces of the Vetch Field and played for Swansea University against the club's mid-week teams which, on one notable occasion, included the mercurial Giorgio Chinaglia at his infuriating worst. Later on, the peerless Ivor Allchurch returned, and to watch him play was one of the great privileges of my life. So great was my attachment to the Vetch that I even took my future wife there on our first date! Over the years I've witnessed the ebb and flow of the fortunes of the club with keen interest and I'm currently writing the official centenary history of the Swans in time for the celebrations in 2012. Few seasons in the history of the club have been as pulsatingly successful as that of 2010–11 and everyone associated with the club, especially the chairman Huw Jenkins, the manager Brendan Rodgers, the entire squad of players and the backroom staff, deserve the highest praise for guiding Swansea City Football Club into the Premiership. I hope they, and the Jack Army, will enjoy reliving the dreams, the precious moments and the extraordinary climax to the season depicted in these pages.

I'm deeply grateful to the club for its support. Special thanks are due to Jonathan Wilsher, Media and Communications Manager, for providing helpful material and for his general interest in the publications on soccer by Y Lolfa.

I'm indebted to the staff of Y Lolfa, especially Lefi Gruffudd (a Swansea Jack through and through), for their full cooperation. My wife Ann, as always, has given me every possible support during the preparation of this book, even to the extent of regularly sitting beside the most fidgety and vocal husband in the East Stand. Being at Wembley together on 30 May 2011 was one of the most unforgettable days of our lives.

Geraint H Jenkins

August 2011

1

The Rise from Near Extinction

R UMOUR HAS IT that it sometimes rains in Swansea. It certainly did on the morning of Bank Holiday Monday, 30 May 2011. In fact, it rained cats and dogs from dawn onwards. Not that any supporters of Swansea City Football Club noticed the dampness. All eyes were on Wembley as a 40,000-strong Jack Army prepared to cheer their favourites to victory against Reading in the play-off final for promotion from the Championship to the coveted Premier League. Not since John Toshack had led his merry men to the dizzy heights of the First Division thirty years earlier had the city buzzed with such excitement. The nerves that had been building up over the previous fortnight were now replaced by a delicious tingle of anticipation. Defeat at the last hurdle was surely unthinkable but, as Huw Jenkins, the wisest of chairmen, put it on the eve of the game: 'I feel excitement, but I'm scared to death. I'm optimistic, but I'm pessimistic!' Supporting Swansea City had always been akin to riding on the hairiest rollercoaster, and he and the fans knew that rich financial rewards, perhaps as much as a bonanza of £90 million, awaited the winner.

As bleary-eyed fans tumbled out of their beds, there was little to be done except to shower and eat a hearty breakfast. Virtually all the preparations for the big day had been completed the previous evening. Black and white suits had been fished out of wardrobes and pressed, replica club shirts had been washed and ironed, black and white wigs had been tried on, and jester's hats, scarves, rosettes, flags and umbrellas had been placed at the ready. Loud sounds of gargling could be heard in bathrooms as fans practised full-throated roars and a few chants of 'Swansea 'til I die'. War paint was the only thing left and the beloved logo of the Swan was carefully transferred on to the eager cheeks of the young and the young-at-heart. The invasion of Wembley was about to begin. Around a sixth of the inhabitants of the city set off either by rail or on the M4 early that morning. As a wonderful banner headline of the

Evening Post put it: 'Will the last person le Swansea on Monday please lock the door?'

Buoyed by a huge wave of excitement, a convoy of flag-bearing vehicles braved the pouring rain. Prawn sandwich eaters left in special trains, while the foot-soldiers clambered on to 77 coaches, many of which had been brought in from England to meet the insatiable demand. Comfort was high on the agenda of those who had spent their savings on hiring stretch limousines (even pink ones) so that they could raise a glass or two as they sped past Cardiff. Saloon cars by the thousands, vans and even motor bikes, many of them festooned with club colours and images of the players, thundered down the motorway. Having queued for long hours for their tickets, fans were determined to enjoy the day. Some very nearly never made it to Wembley. A coach from deepest Ceredigion broke down twice on the M4. A frantic appeal was made on Radio Wales and in a matter of minutes another coach, which was conveniently sitting idle at the Urdd National Eisteddfod in Swansea, was dispatched to rescue the passengers and enable them to tumble into their seats at Wembley a minute before kick-off. An afternoon of heart-stopping drama lay ahead.

No one would have predicted this transformation eight years earlier when, on 3 May 2003, Swansea needed to beat Hull City to avoid slipping out of the Football League, perhaps never to return. For many years the club seemed to have been in a permanent state of crisis and in 2001 it fell into the hands of Tony Petty, a shady Australian-based businessman who, in a very short space of time, became the most widely loathed man in Swansea. With the help of former player and businessman Mel Nurse, known and admired to this day as 'Mr Swansea', Petty was driven out by the sheer power of public opinion. Some semblance of sanity was restored when Brian Flynn was placed in charge of the team in September 2002. He became the club's ninth manager in seven years. Born in Port Talbot, just ten miles from the Vetch Field, Flynn was probably the tiniest manager in the history of the club. But the 'Mighty Flynn' had won the first of his 66 international caps at the Vetch and had been a hugely successful manager and coach at Wrexham. No one was more likely to save the Swans from life in the Nationwide Conference League or possible extinction. On his arrival Swansea were marooned in the 92nd spot, but he kept the club afloat until the last day of the season. The match against Hull was an afternoon of gut-wrenching tension. Alan Curtis, who was assistant manager at the time, confessed that his 'stomach was in knots', though that did not prevent him from making a moving pre-match speech which he still reckons was his finest 'Churchillian moment'. A capacity crowd of 9,585 could barely watch, but the Swans played with great spirit and commitment. A hat-trick by local hero James Thomas was the highlight of the afternoon and there was a great roar of delight and relief when the final whistle signalled a 4–2 victory. Fans swarmed on to the pitch and the celebrations went on long into the night. In the following season, Brian Flynn's team achieved a respectable top-half finish and although he had left by mid-March he will always be remembered not only as one of the saviours of the club but also as the man who brought cult hero Lee Trundle or 'Magic Daps' to Swansea.

The club's chairman Huw Jenkins, who had taken office in 2002, was determined not to repeat the mistakes of the past. Working closely with his fellow-board members and the newly-formed Supporters' Trust, especially Leigh Dineen and Huw Cooze, he produced a prudent business plan and insisted that the club would henceforward live within its means and be accountable to its fans. He was also determined to return to the Swansea way of playing football and entrust the club's future to young and talented managers with attractive personalities, media skills and coaching brains. Flynn had set a good example and his replacement, Kenny Jackett, proved to be another astute young manager.

A one-club player, Jackett had been a tenacious wing half at Watford and had won 31 caps for Wales. He swiftly realized that promotion out of Division Two would depend on old heads and mental toughness. In his view, the hurly-burly at that level was no place for untried youngsters. He rebuilt the team and produced a well-disciplined, gutsy unit. Among his recruits was Garry Monk, who came from Southampton in 2004 and over time became an indispensable figure in Swansea's back-four. A strong disciplinarian, Jackett stamped out some of the worst drinking habits at the club and imposed a tough training regime. In his first season at the helm, Swansea were promoted to Division One and won the FAW Premier Cup. Fans began to flock in growing numbers when the dilapidated Vetch Field was abandoned in 2005 in favour of the handsome new Liberty

Stadium, built on the outskirts of the city and sporting first-class facilities for both football and rugby. At the end the 2005–6 season Jackett came within a whisker of achieving promotion in consecutive seasons following an agonizing 3–4 penalty shoot-out in a play-off final against Barnsley at the Millennium Stadium in Cardiff. Yet in that same season the club won both the Football League Trophy and the FAW Premier Cup.

The board had every faith in Jackett and he might have achieved even greater success had he also managed to win the hearts of the fans. He had assembled a strong, physical team that played football the Watford way by getting the ball forward quickly and using a good deal of aerial power. But this was not the Swansea way and, dismayed by the barrage of catcalls from home supporters, Jackett unexpectedly handed in his notice in February 2007. He had stabilized the club, instilled a winning mentality into the players, and achieved an excellent 44.23 per cent win rate ratio over the best part of three seasons. He, like Flynn, deserved high praise.

Then came an inspired appointment. Roberto Martinez, a former player with silky midfield skills, took over the managerial reins on 23

February the same year and began transforming the playing style. 'El Gaffer', as the swarthy young Catalan was popularly known, believed that football was a form of art. The ball itself was a treasured possession, to be confiscated and caressed for most of the game. One-touch passing, speed on the flanks, and collective understanding became the basis of a new and exciting game-plan based on a 4–3–3 formation. Martinez signed a new crop of young and intelligent players, several of them from Spain and Holland, whom he described as being 'hungry to win honours with their new club and enthusiastic about football'. Bewildered opponents simply could not get the ball as Martinez's men passed and probed patiently. By the end of the 2007–8 season the team had romped to the League One title. At times the football was mesmerizing.

By the time Swansea finished eighth in the Championship in 2008–9 Martinez had become a much-loved Jack, regularly serenaded by doting followers at the Liberty Stadium. In his autobiography, *Kicking Every Ball*, he spoke glowingly of his love for Swansea and Wales. 'In Roberto we trust' was the cry among the supporters and he responded by declaring that he would never leave unless the board chose to force him out. This statement made him a hostage to fortune and one that he would deeply regret when, out of the blue, he joined his old club Wigan on 15 June 2009, leaving the supporters angry and heartbroken by what they believed to be an act of unforgivable betrayal. Martinez underestimated the depth of ill-feeling his desertion would cause and although Huw Jenkins, who emerged from the whole sorry affair with his dignity intact, made conciliatory noises, the board's plans for the future had been cruelly disrupted.

Undaunted, Jenkins turned to another handsome and sophisticated Iberian. The snazzily dressed Paulo Sousa, recently sacked for some mysterious indiscretion by Queens Park Rangers, turned up for his first press conference as if auditioning for a Hollywood film. With 51 Portuguese caps to his name as well as a wealth of playing experience with Inter Milan, Juventus and Borussia Dortmund, he had all the right credentials except perhaps a deep knowledge of players in the Football League. In spite of the upheaval caused by the departure of Martinez, Sousa promised to carry on with the club's master plan and, with only modest financial resources at his disposal, he managed in a very short space of time to knit his players together into an effective unit. Keeping possession of the ball remained an overriding priority, but Sousa also rebranded the team by establishing a sounder defensive shape. His team played tidy, watchable but often unthreatening football. As Lee Trundle admitted, 'We'd be too reluctant to go for it in games'. There were few thrills and spills in the penalty box and during the 2009–10 season Swansea managed to score only 40 league goals. Yet, the club finished the season only a point adrift of the play-offs in a very creditable seventh position, its best performance for 27 years. The board's long-term plan was clearly bearing fruit. But then, as in the case of Martinez, Sousa left abruptly in the close season for a richer club, this time Leicester City. His defensive pragmatism had not pleased those many fans who yearned for more flair and adventure. Yet he undoubtedly left the club on a stronger footing. The story of progress and evolution continued.

By mid-July 2010 the Welsh media had led the public to believe that Gary Speed would be Sousa's successor, but Huw Jenkins had a different card to play. Unlike his Portuguese predecessor, the new appointee Brendan Rodgers, a native of Carnlough, a small village in County Antrim in Northern Ireland, was not a former international star or even a household name. His modest playing career had been cut short by injury at the age of twenty and in November 2009 he had been dismissed as manager of Reading after just six months in post. But Rodgers had been one of Jose Mourinho's brightest coaches at Chelsea in 2004–6 and was believed to be the ideal man to introduce a bolder and more attacking approach. Huw Jenkins and his board members were certainly impressed by his vision for the future and were mindful of the fact that his coaching experience stretched over seventeen years. A calm, affable and studious man, Rodgers had mapped out a future which fitted the Swansea mould. In his own words: 'My philosophy is to play creative, attacking football with tactical discipline, but you have to validate that with success.' Adept at filling his players with self-belief, he had a more touchy-feely approach than the aloof Sousa and immediately established a warm rapport with the team and the general public. Under his management, the club seemed destined to take a major step forward. But, as the 2010–11 season loomed, the unanswered question on many lips was: could this largely untried 37-year-old guide the club into the fantasy land the fans had dreamed of for so long?

2

The 2010–11 Squad

THE SWANSEA SQUAD, and the style it adopted in 2010–11, had evolved over a period of six years. It contained outstandingly skilful players and some rugged ones too. All of them were comfortable on the ball and capable of passing it quickly and accurately. No one dived or cheated, harangued referees or brought the game into disrepute. By letting their football speak for itself, under Brendan Rodgers the Swans became the most attractive team in the Championship. It was also a cosmopolitan outfit. Thirty years earlier, when John Toshack had led the ambitious thrust for promotion to the top tier, the backbone of his squad were Welsh players, supported by a strong Merseyside presence (is not Liverpool part of north Wales?) and a couple of Slavs. But Rodgers's players reflected the global nature of the professional game and supporters of the club no longer derided Johnny Foreigner. Indeed, they knew full well that mounting a convincing promotion campaign depended on the club's ability to buy affordable players from countries other than Wales to augment home-grown talent. The 2010–11 squad was therefore composed of players from Belgium, England, Holland, Ireland, Italy, Scotland, Spain and Wales.

Every successful team needs a good and reliable goalkeeper, and in Dorus de Vries, who was signed by Martinez from Dunfermline in 2007, the club secured a brave and competitive custodian. A former Den Haag player, with Under-21 caps for Holland to his name, he proved to be one of the most mentally tough players on the staff. An accomplished shot-stopper, he kept clean sheets in 25 games under Sousa. But his main gift was his ability to control and direct play from his own penalty area. He never punted long, aimless balls upfield. An excellent kicker and thrower of the ball, he unerringly found the nearest unmarked player, thereby allowing the team to build from the back. His Achilles heel was in-swinging corners, but he remained confident and competitive in every game. Since de Vries remained virtually injury-free during the 2010–11 season, his understudy Yves Makabu-Makalambay, an astonishingly tall native of Belgium who was capped by the Democratic Republic of Congo, was given few opportunities, while the up-and-coming David Cornell, an Under-21 Welsh international, was loaned to Port Talbot over the season as part of his footballing education.

The system adopted by the club meant that the full-backs were expected to attack speedily down the flanks. In Angel Rangel, who cost a mere £10,000, Martinez found a real gem. Formerly a part-timer with lowly Terrassa in Segunda B, the third level of the Spanish football league system, Rangel was arguably the classiest member of the playing staff. Stronger going forward than in the tackle, he was technically sound, a superb passer of the ball and a tireless overlapper. His name was a godsend to specialists in *cynghanedd*, a form of poetic rhyme in Welsh and, as one sports commentator enthused, 'Is there a finer name in the entire football league than Angel Rangel?' On the opposite flank, St Asaph-born Neil Taylor had been snapped up from Wrexham in the summer of 2010. Although still only 21, he was a Welsh international with huge potential. A natural left-back, Taylor had the pace and athleticism to launch counter-attacks as well as tenacity in the tackle. From an attacking point of view, his ability to drift inwards and outwards and to interchange with the predominantly right-footed winger Scott Sinclair was a great asset.

At the heart of a generally well-organized defence was club captain Garry Monk, whom Kenny Jackett had signed on a free transfer from Southampton in 2004. Over the years Monk proved his leadership qualities time and again. His vast experience, never-say-die approach and astute reading of the game meant that the extent of his influence was never more noticeable than when injury kept him out of the side. Like so many other veterans at the club over the years, he had become a Swansea man through and through. In his regular programme notes, he unfailingly urged supporters to be loud, proud and positive. Although the cumulative effect of serious injuries meant that he was sometimes caught out by his lack of real pace, he was always a steadying influence, and there was no one better at coaxing and chivvying referees. At his side was the trustiest of centre-backs Ashley Williams, a Welsh international signed by Martinez from lowly Stockport. Williams did not miss a single league game over three seasons, a remarkable record for a defender. He was strong and competitive, and his long-range passing, especially with his left foot, as well as his surges into midfield, were an added bonus. He would also develop an unexpected knack of scoring goals, though not all of them ended up in opponents' nets.

Two other tough and aggressive centre-backs waited in the wings. Long-serving Geordie Alan Tate had initially come on loan from Manchester United in 2003. Initially combustible and reckless, he had matured into an extremely versatile and reliable defender whose bone-jarring tackles and heroic blocks either at full-back or centre-back made him a local hero. Although Albert Serran, signed from Espanyol by Martinez in 2008, was not the swiftest of defenders, he too was a rugged tackler whose wondrous physique earned him the nickname 'the Terminator'. Much quicker was Ashley or 'Jazz' Richards, a versatile full-back and midfielder who had come up through the ranks and captained the Wales Under-21 team. He and Sketty-born Daniel Alfei, another hungry young home-grown player, were certainly ones for the future, as were the likes of Joe Walsh and Casey Thomas.

Given that the system honed and developed over the years depended on retaining possession in midfield, it is not surprising that some of the club's finest footballers patrolled the middle third of the pitch. Significantly, managers Flynn, Jackett, Martinez and Sousa had all been intelligent midfield players. They knew, and so did Rodgers, that controlling that vitally important space was the key to success and Swansea's promotion bid owed a good deal to the way in which a group of skilful players managed to dominate possession of the ball and distribute it quickly and effectively.

Pride of place must go to Joe Allen. He was an exceptional talent. Born in Carmarthen and raised in Pembrokeshire, he had been with the club since the age of eight. In a cosmopolitan dressing room he was the only fluent Welsh-speaker. Still only 21, he had come to epitomize the skill and spirit in the squad. His sureness of touch, crisp passing and phenomenal energy made him a favourite with the spectators. Small but strong, he was not easily knocked off the ball and he played every game with a determined glint in his eye. Brendan Rodgers admiringly dubbed him 'the Welsh Xavi' and the young midfielder could look forward to winning far more than the two caps to his name.

Even smaller – but just as gifted – was

playmaker Leon Britton, who returned to the club in January 2011 after a short sabbatical with Sheffield United, whom he had joined after publicly falling out with Sousa over contractual matters. The quality of football at the Liberty, at least in midfield, had been diminished by his absence. Swansea fans had adored him ever since he arrived in 2002 and the cry 'Leon!' rang out often in the Liberty Stadium as the little fellow displayed his wonderful skills. Few players in the Championship could dictate the rhythm of play as well as Britton. His touch, control and composure, as well as his ability to tidy up the errors of his colleagues, made him the heartbeat of the team.

Essex-born Darren Pratley was a very different type of player. Tall, powerful and athletic, he was the best trainer at the club. Signed from Fulham for a fee of £100,000 in 2006, he always showed great endeavour and tenacity. His raking stride and stamina took him from box to box, and over time his goal-scoring record improved markedly. Few midfielders at Swansea could match him for sweetly-struck volleys, the most famous of which was his winner against rivals Cardiff in November 2009.

The only naturally left-sided player in the

middle of the park was the Catalan Andrea Orlandi, a former winger bought by Martinez from Alaves in 2007. Sousa had converted him into a stylish midfielder whose elegant left foot introduced variety at set-pieces. Although he lacked firepower in front of goal, Orlandi fitted in well with Swansea's free-flowing style of play, and until his season was blighted by injuries there were signs that he was adding a touch of steel to his game.

Another former winger reinvented himself, or was reinvented, as a holding midfielder. Mark Gower had arrived from Southend in 2008 with a reputation as a free-scoring flanker, but it turned out that luck seldom favoured him whenever he shot for goal. Posts, crossbars, the occasional corner flag were all struck on a regular basis and even his finest efforts seemed to bring out the best in opposing goalkeepers. Shrewdly, Sousa moved him into midfield where his clever feet and strong running could leave their mark. Even at 32, Gower brought vibrancy and passion into the midfield as well as chirpy banter to the dressing room.

Then there was the enigma known as Germain or Kemy Agustien, a highly-rated former Under-21 international Dutch midfielder whom Rodgers signed on a two-year contract in October 2010. A strapping defensive midfielder who was hard to outmuscle, he was brought in to add a touch of aggression as well as long-range passing options. But previous and pre-season injuries had taken their toll and as the season progressed he had few opportunities to prove his worth. Loaned to Crystal Palace in the latter stages, he showed signs of recovering his form and of becoming a linchpin in coming seasons.

Another gifted defensive midfielder was the former Real Madrid and Sevilla player Jordi Lopez, an expensive recruit whom Sousa had signed in the summer of 2009. Although he was a tenacious player with excellent passing skills, for some mysterious reason the Swansea fans did not warm to him. He made only twenty appearances, including four under Rodgers, until his contract was cancelled by mutual consent in mid-January 2011.

Last but not least among these gifted midfielders was Sean MacDonald, a 21-year-old Swansea lad with a mop of ginger hair and an old head on his shoulders. Having won 25 caps for Wales at Under-21 level and a full cap against Switzerland in October 2010, he was a player worth nurturing. According to Alan Curtis, few were able to rob him of the ball in small-sided games on the training field. Between 2009 and 2011 he spent several spells learning his trade at Yeovil and always returned a better and a wiser player, as indeed did young Scott Donnelly, who was loaned to Wycombe Wanderers.

But, as the careers of international stars like Cliff Jones and Leighton James had shown, the Swansea way had always encouraged pace on the flanks. Brendan Rodgers was a strong believer in using quicksilver wingers and had no intention of asking them, as Sousa had done, to spend large amounts of time tracking back and defending. Nathan Dyer, who was signed for a fee of £400,000 from Southampton by Martinez in June 2009, was the nearest thing to Lionel Messi at the Liberty Stadium. Dyer simply loved playing football and delighted in leading hapless full-backs a merry dance. His technical skill, pace and trickery won the hearts of the fans and if only that mischievous sparkle in his eyes could help him score more goals he would be a world-beater. Rodgers gave him free rein to express his outrageous talent and, by a masterstroke, found him an equally scintillating partner on the left flank. Bath-born Scott Sinclair had been one of his protégés at Chelsea and was an England Under-21 international. A widely-travelled loanee, he was signed from Chelsea for a bargain fee in August 2010. Sinclair combined devastating speed and trickery with a remarkable knack of scoring goals. On his day, he was irresistible.

Their understudies were also gifted footballers. David Cotterill, a Welsh international whom Sousa signed from Sheffield United, was a stylish runner with a sweet first touch and a fierce shot. Frustrated by the lack of opportunities, he was loaned to Portsmouth for the latter months of the season. The former Ajax winger Cedric van der Gun was also an experienced campaigner who made up for his lack of speed by snapping up unlikely goal-scoring opportunities.

One of the major problems which faced both Sousa and Rodgers was how to replace the free-scoring Jason Scotland who had followed Martinez to Wigan, only to find himself warming the bench at the DW Stadium and yearning for the Mumbles. His ability to hold the ball up, as well as his goal-scoring prowess, had not been adequately replaced and under Sousa's watch the team managed to score only 40 goals during the 2009–10 season. Hopes had been raised when Craig Beattie, a Scotland international at

West Bromwich Albion, was signed by Sousa for a record fee of £500,000 rising to £800,000. Wholehearted in his play, desperate to succeed and hugely popular with his colleagues, Beattie nevertheless remained as injury-prone as his previous record had suggested he would be. Yet, when given the opportunity, he showed not only how to score goals but also how to celebrate in true Benny Hill fashion.

Other strikers either inherited or signed by Rodgers did not measure up to expectations. The rampaging Gorka Pintado's chief claim to fame was to flatten Robbie Savage with an eye-watering tackle during an ill-tempered match at Derby. Shefti Kuqi, a Finland international, was a highly intelligent footballer, but he was clearly beginning to feel the burdens of the passing years. Even the experienced striker Luke Moore, who arrived from West Bromwich Albion for an undisclosed fee in January 2011, took time to settle. The striker most likely to score was Stephen Dobbie, whom Martinez had lured from Queen of the South to the Liberty Stadium shortly before he left for the Latics. Sousa did not rate him highly and he was loaned to Blackpool. Sod's law meant that Dobbie inevitably helped to ensure that Blackpool reached the play-offs at Swansea's expense and eventually win promotion. On his return to Swansea, however, Rodgers filled him with self-belief. He worked on the Scot's first touch and improved his ability to bring others into the game. Most of all, he encouraged him to shoot on sight. Dobbie's piledrivers would prove to be one of the wonders of the season.

Then, quite unexpectedly, Rodgers waved his magic wand once more. In mid-March 2011 he persuaded Chelsea to let him borrow Fabio Borini, a born striker who, at the tender age of 20, was already being courted by leading clubs in Serie A. Like Jason Scotland, he was comfortable in receiving the ball while facing his own goal, but, unlike Scotland, his movement off the ball was also extremely impressive, as was his hunger for goals. Borini adapted quickly to the rigours of the Championship, had plenty of fire in his belly, and wore the Swansea shirt with pride.

There were also two long-term casualties who deserve mention. Tom Butler, a wisecracking Dubliner with two caps for the Republic of Ireland on his CV, had been signed from Hartlepool by Kenny Jackett in July 2006. He was a winger with an exquisite first touch and the balance of a ballet dancer. Troubled by a serious thigh injury, however, he played no part in the drive for promotion in the 2010–11 season except insofar as his quips made the dressing room a happier place. Another long-standing casualty was Ferrie Bodde, formerly of Den Haag and a midfielder of the highest quality. An aggressive enforcer – often called the 'Evil Genius'– his distribution was immaculate and his long-range shooting quite devastating. A career-threatening knee injury in November 2008, however, meant that a long period of rehabilitation lay before him and it was to the club's great credit that steps were taken to renew his contract as he set his sights on returning to the fray in the 2011–12 season.

Many incoming managers dispense with existing assistant managers or coaches at their new clubs. Brendan Rodgers was much wiser. Aware that Swansea's strength was its community base and that the fans warmly cherished former heroes, he was glad to retain the services of Alan Curtis and Colin Pascoe. Even though he was a Rhondda boy, no one epitomized the Swansea spirit more than Curtis. Ever since he took lodgings as an apprentice in the home of the legendary Harry Griffiths in the early seventies, he had become an adopted Jack. 'I have loved every minute I have spent here,' he wrote in his autobiography. This many-talented striker had three spells with the club, scoring 72 goals in 248 games, winning 35 caps for Wales, and starring in the promotion-winning team in 1981. He even took his wedding vows in the shadow of his beloved Vetch Field. When Rodgers appointed him first-team coach at the beginning of the 2010–11 season, the sprightly 56-year-old still looked as if he could hold his own in Championship matches.

Colin Pascoe was just as committed to the Swansea cause. Formerly a swift and direct left winger, this Port Talbot boy came to prominence in the Toshack era. Although he later had spells with Sunderland and Blackpool, his heart was always with Swansea. He scored 54 goals in 270 league games for the Swans and one of the highlights of his career was his starring role in the victory in the 1994 Autoglass Windshield Trophy final at Wembley. He deserved more than his ten Welsh caps. On retirement he took up coaching and played an important role in bringing on fresh talent and in displaying a shrewd tactical brain. Rodgers cared about those who cared about Swansea, and he happily appointed him assistant manager. He had no cause to regret either appointment.

Like most rising stars on the managerial circuit, Rodgers was also aware of the benefits of sports science and meticulous analytical preparation. Two backroom appointments strengthened his hand in this direction. Ryland Morgans was appointed to supervise levels of fitness and conditioning, and to offer expert advice on nutrition and rehabilitation methods. Chris Davies, an expert in performance analysis, was brought in to prepare detailed statistical information on forthcoming opponents as well as on the attainments of Swansea players in each game.

Rodgers had little time to run the rule over his squad, but three pre-season games in Holland allowed him to impress on his players that his main priority would be to secure maximum commitment from each one of them within the framework of the team. Soccer is a game of risks and rewards and, unlike Sousa, Rodgers urged his players from the outset to take the initiative, force the pace and make things happen. Pace and penetration would be his watchwords. But, wise enough to play down the over-excitement in the local press, he sounded a note of caution about Swansea's prospects. To finish in the top ten, he claimed, would be an outstanding achievement for a club which could not match the financial resources of its main rivals. Privately, however, he must surely have reckoned that improving on Sousa's achievement in finishing in seventh spot in the league was feasible. There was certainly cause for muted optimism.

One thing was certain. The players had every faith in their new manager. 'He talks to every one of us,' said captain Garry Monk, 'not just about football but about everything in your life and things in his life.' Success in football does not always depend on what happens on the field of play and Brendan Rodgers's deeply ingrained moral compass imbued his players with a strong sense of responsibility for the club and the community. The manager also appreciated the commitment and support of his players and never made the mistake of criticizing any of them in public. Indeed, he praised them openly: 'I come into work every day and I am very proud to lead this group of men and this team. They give their all and they have great ambition, not only for themselves but for the group and for the club.'

Third Spot by Christmas

With 46 league fixtures to be played in the nine months ahead of them, no Swansea follower was surprised to discover that the first of them was an away tie at Hull City. Since 2005 the club had been drawn away in the first match of every season and had lost every one of them. Such early-season travel sickness was puzzling and on 7 August the team once more returned empty-handed after a disappointingly limp performance. A wonderful first-half strike by John Bostock and a close range half-volley by Ian Ashbee in the second half sealed Swansea's fate against one of the favourites for promotion. It was all too predictable and the 1,141 travelling fans were especially dismayed to find that Swansea created so few chances.

Although Rodgers was disappointed by the

outcome, his faith in his philosophy did not waver. Sousa would have spent the following week plugging defensive gaps and instructing his forwards to work back, but Rodgers bolstered the attack and boosted morale by using his Chelsea connections to bring in a highly rated winger with not only pace and dribbling ability but also a deadly eye for goal. Scott Sinclair – clean-cut, assured and supremely talented – had played under Mourinho, Scolari, Hiddink and Ancelotti, and was destined for great things. To have signed him for less than a million pounds in total was a major coup by the manager. With him in the team there was no likelihood of Swansea scoring just 40 league goals in the season.

Yet, there was a sombre air around the Liberty Stadium when Sinclair made his debut at home to Preston a week later. This was the first opportunity for the public to express their sorrowful tribute to the late Besian Idrizaj, a promising young Austrian forward who had died in his sleep in his native land in mid-May. Thousands of fans held up cards and scarves in tribute to the young striker and a prominent banner bore the words: 'Always in our heart, always a Jack.' This poignant demonstration of loss by the players and the supporters alike inspired the team to produce a performance of rare quality. Preston were thrashed 4–0. Playing almost a 4–2–4 system, with Cotterill filling the hole behind Dobbie, the team showed in abundance the pace and penetration the manager had promised. Three goals in the first half by Dobbie, Pratley and Dyer ripped an admittedly woeful Preston apart, and a second-half penalty by Cotterill – the first of four won by Dyer during the season – sealed their fate. 'Football is meant to be fun,' claimed a beaming Dyer afterwards and the hard-running pressure which he and his fellow-winger Sinclair had imposed had helped to open up Preston. Fitting in well in his role as a midfield general, Mark Gower was at the heart of many of Swansea's best moves and the crowd of over 14,000 were treated to a fine display of direct, passing football.

Within a week the Swans were at Carrow Road, this time with only 315 travelling supporters to cheer them on. Having weathered an early storm, the team settled down and over the course of the game retained 60 per cent of possession. The home crowd, even the voluble Delia Smith, fell silent as the visitors controlled the pattern of play. Then, after 82 minutes, came a critical turning point which worked in

Norwich's favour. The speedy Sinclair zipped through the middle, only to be felled by Ruddy, the Norwich goalkeeper, in the penalty box. Inexplicably, Ruddy was allowed to stay on the field as Cotterill stepped up to take the penalty. His shot was well struck, but Ruddy, diving to his right, got his hand to the ball and diverted it to safety. Worse was to follow. With three minutes left, Ashley Williams poked a cross flashing in from the left into his own net and a brilliant volley by Simeon Jackson in the closing seconds sealed the points for Norwich. Swansea had dominated the game but had spurned a host of golden chances. Poor Cotterill was inconsolable, but Swansea's overall performance meant that there was little cause for alarm.

The last league fixture in August, a home match against newly-relegated Burnley, was a hotly-contested affair in which Swansea maintained a high tempo throughout. Monk and Williams marshalled the defence with steely vigour and wingers Dyer and Sinclair made life a misery for the visitors' full-backs. Swansea's pressing game forced Burnley back, and even when Pratley had been sent off for a second bookable offence in the 58th minute, the home side maintained an irresistible momentum. The winning goal, when it came, was an absolute gem. An increasingly wobbly Burnley defence failed to cope with a scintillating six-man move which Sinclair joyously finished. Late pressure applied by Burnley jangled a few nerves, but it was not enough to salvage a point. Confidence was growing, home support was increasing and pundits were warming to the new style of play.

But there were to be no easy rides in this league and September brought mixed fortunes. A visit to Elland Road is an intimidating experience at the best of times, but in the early stages Swansea played with great imagination and courage. After 13 minutes they went ahead when Dobbie fired home from eight yards. The passing was swift and cohesive, but Leeds stormed back in the second half and bullied the Swans into conceding two goals and the match. With 13 minutes left, referee Grant Hegley, who had denied Swansea a blatant penalty in the crucial last home fixture against Doncaster in the previous season, waved away strong appeals for a spot-kick when Joe Allen surged into the box and was brought down. After that, there was to be no comeback. Leeds dropped the pace of the game and made off with the spoils.

Fortunately, home results remained impeccable. Three days after the defeat at Leeds, the return of Pratley stiffened the midfield in a clash against a robust, unlovely Coventry team bent on making as many shuddering tackles as the referee would allow. Undaunted, Swansea stormed forward in an outstanding display of attacking football. With Allen at the hub of things and Dyer at his tricky best, the sheer speed and off-the-ball running of the home team overwhelmed Coventry. Goals by Pratley and Sinclair were the highlights as the visitors, struggling to make any impression, sat deep and hoped for the best. On the following Saturday, lowly Scunthorpe were just as stubborn and it took 80 minutes to break down their resistance. Commanding 55 per cent of possession, the Swans probed patiently as the Lincolnshire men sought to squeeze the life out of the game. Fortune favours the brave, and two decisive changes by Rodgers broke the stalemate. Cotterill and Dobbie were brought on to test the tiring visitors' defence. On 83 minutes a sparkling run and cross by Cotterill paved the way for a goal by Sinclair and two minutes later the trusty Dobbie sealed the victory with an emphatic strike from eight yards.

Two successive home wins catapulted Swansea into sixth place and spirits were high as the team bus headed to the City Ground at

Nottingham. But here, of all places, the team produced its poorest display of the season. Nothing seemed to go right. The home side were in fine form and rattled the Swans with their swift tackling and speedy counter-attacks which brought them three goals against an increasingly ragged defence. Without the injured Sinclair and Dobbie, the visitors lacked penetration and a late goal from close range by van der Gun was scant consolation. With eight league games played, Swansea had suffered four away defeats against teams who had realistic hopes of winning automatic promotion.

Then, as if to silence the critics, the Swans bounced back by embarking on an unbeaten seven-match run in the league. Nearly 600 fans travelled to Watford on 28 September for a mid-week fixture against Brendan Rodgers's former team, now managed by his firm friend Malky Mackay. Watford were no mean team, but from the outset there was a steely resolve about Swansea's play. It was as if the players were determined not to let the manager down in his old stamping ground. Goals by Sinclair, Dobbie and Frank Nouble, a young striker on loan from West Ham, stunned the home fans as Swansea raced into a three-goal lead. Watford came back strongly by scoring twice towards the end and only the assistant referee's flag prevented them from equalizing at the death. But the Swans were worthy winners and one could sense that, having laid the away bogey to rest, they really did believe that their style of play could bring success at home and away.

As the Swans set themselves on an upward path, visiting teams sought to counter their progress by defending in numbers. A scoreless mid-week draw at home to an unambitious Derby County on 2 October was not the end of the world. After all, home fans were able to celebrate Alan Tate's 300th appearance and seize every opportunity to boo and heckle everyone's favourite pantomime villain Robbie Savage. Had Sinclair been fit to play, Swansea might have stretched the visiting defence to breaking point, but wars of attrition of this kind are never satisfying either for the players or the crowd. None the less, now in eighth spot, with sixteen points in the bag, the Swans were handily placed.

Rodgers was determined to persist with his adventurous approach as he returned to another of his former haunts at the Madejski Stadium on 16 October. Some 2,199 expectant fans had made the journey and were in good voice. Raiding swiftly down the flanks, the Swans carved out several sumptuous openings and were rewarded in the 35th minute when Cotterill slipped a perfect pass through to Sinclair who rounded the keeper and finished the move expertly. Although Swansea were by far the better team, there was no triumphalism from Rodgers. The victory was deeply satisfying, but he bore no grudges against his former employers and was too decent a man to crow in the company of many old friends or in the ensuing press conference.

Having moved up to fourth place, three days later the Swans pitted their wits against the seemingly runaway leaders Queens Park Rangers in a midweek match at the Liberty Stadium. A strangely subdued crowd of 16,742, the largest home gate to date, witnessed a hotly contested but goalless game in which seven players were booked. With the wily old fox Neil Warnock in charge of the team, the visitors gave no quarter and their physical approach knocked Swansea out of their stride in the early stages. Yet this was a game which they could and should have won. Once more the unfortunate Cotterill was found wanting when a penalty was awarded after 38 minutes. His tame effort was saved by Paddy Kenny and thereafter he rarely figured in league matches as Rodgers replaced him with on-loan Martin Emnes, a lithe and skilful Dutch winger from Middlesbrough and, later on, used Dobbie in the hole behind the main striker. The manager may have suspected that Cotterill, for all his undoubted talent on the ball, possibly lacked mental toughness at key stages in a game. From then on penalties were entrusted to, and dispatched by, the imperturbable Sinclair.

Elsewhere, previous managers of Swansea were having a torrid time. Under Martinez, Wigan were seemingly bound for relegation and, after just three months in post, Paulo Sousa was sacked by Leicester City for his sterile tactics and for losing the respect of the players. His replacement was the widely travelled international manager Sven-Göran Eriksson, a celebrity in his own right and charged with the task of winning promotion. It was his misfortune to come to Swansea on 23 October and find that the home team had no intention of helping him achieve that aim. From the first whistle, the Swans were in complete control. Even the experienced Swede was deeply impressed by the flowing moves set up by Swansea and the way in which their midfield players snapped into tackles and won the ball back so swiftly. In the 49th minute Pratley sent Marvin Emnes through and the little Dutchman was strong enough to hold off challengers before driving the ball high into the net. With Allen constantly in the thick of things, Pratley winning important tackles and Dyer at his brilliant best, Leicester were hard pushed to stay in the game. And when Agustien, who replaced Orlandi after 69 minutes, broke Leicester's hearts by winning the ball even more aggressively and spraying passes to his team's marauding wingers, there was no way back for them. A tap-in by Sinclair in added time rounded off the most polished and satisfying home performance to date. Almost without notice, the Swans had slipped into third place and had reactivated speculation about promotion.

A week later, nearly a thousand home fans travelled to struggling Crystal Palace to see whether the intense competitiveness shown in recent weeks was as strong as ever. Once more Joe Allen was the dominant influence in midfield, overshadowing the experienced Dutchman Edgar Davids and stamping his authority on the game from the outset. A goal by Sinclair, his eleventh of the season in all competitions, settled nerves in the sixth minute, and goals by Pratley and Allen in the second half were nothing more than the Swans deserved against a plucky but outclassed side. Goalkeeper Dorus de Vries in particular had every reason to be satisfied: this was his fifth clean sheet in succession.

Even as the referee's final whistle blew at Crystal Palace, thoughts were turning to the next fixture, a long-awaited away clash in six days time against old rivals Cardiff City who, having beaten Norwich at home, were now sitting proudly at the top of the Championship. There is nothing like a derby for sharpening inter-city rivalries. Reporters on the staff of the *Western Mail* and the *Evening Post* went into overdrive and even some hacks beyond Wales sensed that something special was afoot. With the league leaders in rampant goal-scoring form and Swansea not having conceded a goal in seven and a half hours' play, an epic struggle lay ahead. The pre-match contrast between the attitudes of the two managers was striking. A downbeat Dave Jones claimed that, even though his side were marginal favourites, he never enjoyed derby games or gave them any priority. By contrast, Rodgers oozed enthusiasm and marvelled at the passion such games engendered among his club's supporters. With Sky Sports cameras at the ground for the lunch-time kick-off, there was every prospect of a rip-roaring encounter in front of a capacity crowd

'El Gaffer': Roberto Martinez

Roberto Martinez, manager of Wigan, is welcomed back to the Liberty Stadium by Brendan Rodgers

Paulo Sousa, immaculately dressed, on the touchline in his last game – Swansea v Doncaster – as manager

Dorus de Vries, goalkeeper extraordinary, celebrates after his swansong at Wembley

The local derby against Cardiff fires up Alan Tate

Captain Marvel: Garry Monk celebrates after the 1-0 victory over Cardiff

Defiance personified: Ashley Williams

Angel Rangel celebrates
his spectacular equalizer
at Doncaster

'There's only one
Joey Allen'

Darren Pratley celebrates scoring with a trademark volley against Crystal Palace

Having scored at Middlesbrough, impish Nathan Dyer gives Scott Sinclair a piggy-back

Stephen Dobbie, scorer of many thunderbolts, celebrates another against Sheffield United

Fabio Borini stuns Norwich with an extraordinary free-kick

'Yes, it's me!' An incredulous Mark Gower celebrates his incredible goal against Norwich

The Four Tops: Luke Moore, Fabio Borini, Ashley Williams and Neil Taylor get into the swing of things against Ipswich

The Jack Army in full voice during the first leg of the play-off semi-finals at the City Ground, Nottingham

Touchline celebrations, with Brendan Rodgers and Colin Pascoe leading the way, as Darren Pratley makes it 3-1 against Nottingham Forest at the Liberty Stadium

Just some of the 40,000-strong Jack Army at Wembley

Reading fans sit in silence as Scott Sinclair tucks away his first penalty at Wembley

More silence behind the goal after Scott Sinclair slots home his second goal

Scott Sinclair is buried by his colleagues after scoring his hat-trick

Amid the celebrations, the late Besian Idrizaj is remembered by the players

Everyone sings 'Hymns and Arias'

The players receive the Championship play-off final trophy at Wembley

The three veterans – Alan Tate, Garry Monk and Leon Britton – hold the play-off cup aloft

The proud manager: Brendan Rodgers hoists the play-off trophy

Brendan Rodgers gets the Guardiola treatment

Garry Monk and Alan Tate on the victory bus parade

'There's only one team in Wales'

Brendan Rodgers teaches Cyril the Swan to chant 'We are Premier League!'

of 26,049, including 1,820 raucous fans from Swansea.

Tactically, Rodgers won the day. Jones unwisely departed from his favoured 4–4–2 system and, by leaving out winger Burke and moving goal-poacher Chopra to the flank, he surrendered the initiative to Swansea. All over the field, Swansea won individual battles. Rangel subdued Bellamy, Allen outran Olofinjana and stood up to some appalling tackles by Chopra, and Emnes outfoxed Gyepes. Everyone had expected a close tussle, but Swansea were demonstrably the better team and superior in every department. The home side were reduced to four shots on target, while Swansea fired thirteen shots at goalkeeper Heaton, one of which settled the tie. It came in the 75th minute when Emnes, having tricked Gyepes into trying to nick the ball on the edge of the box, engineered enough space to rifle a fierce left-foot shot into the bottom corner. Amid joyous celebrations in West Glamorgan after the game, Dave Jones made few friends by depicting Swansea as a team whose centre-backs spent the game passing to each other 'so it doesn't hurt you'. Bragging rights had gone to Wales's second city and the festivities went on long into the night.

Perhaps the festivities went on too long because a rude awakening occurred on the following Wednesday. Bristol City were the visitors and were in no mood to succumb meekly. Swansea started sluggishly and found themselves a goal down after five minutes. Rodgers had rested a few regulars and by the time Allen and Gower had been brought into the fray Bristol had fallen back in numbers to protect their lead. No amount of huffing and puffing could budge them and the West Country side escaped over the Severn Bridge with maximum points. On the following Sunday visitors Middlesbrough were just as dogged. It proved to be one of the few games in which Swansea surrendered overall possession to their opponents. A host of chances were spurned and then, with just about everyone settling for a tame and disappointing draw, in the 84th minute Sinclair cut in from the left and beat goalkeeper Steele with a low but saveable shot which crept in at the near post. Three points kept Swansea in third place.

South Yorkshire was the venue on 20 November. Matches at the Keepmoat Stadium in Doncaster are always awkward affairs and the mood was subdued as the team bus set off without the injured Monk and the suspended Tate. Albert Serran filled the captain's berth and Neil Taylor slotted in at left-back. No one was surprised when the Swans fell behind after 16 minutes and only some marvellous saves by de Vries kept them in the hunt against a team also renowned for attractive football. But, driven on by Allen and Gower, and invigorated by substitute Agustien, they pressed hard for an equalizer. With added time looming, Angel Rangel, who had made many lung-bursting sorties down the right flank, ventured forward once more and deftly controlled a wonderful diagonal pass by Agustien before driving the ball high into the Doncaster net. A 1–1 draw was a fair result, but it had been a mighty close-run thing.

Unexpectedly Swansea then lost at home in an evening match to a streetwise and niggly Portsmouth in front of 17,584 people, the largest home gate to date. The early signs were promising. Within 98 seconds Swansea were ahead. Following a sublime, four-man passing move, Craig Beattie scored his first goal in more than a year. But Portsmouth wormed their way back into the game by scrapping for every ball, committing foul upon foul, contesting every refereeing decision which went against them, and throwing forward their big defenders at set pieces. The injured Monk was badly missed.

Serran could not cope at the heart of the defence, and it was no surprise when Nugent equalized before half-time. During a scrappy second half there was an air of unpleasantness about the play. Portsmouth did not allow Swansea to play their normal game and several of their stalwarts, led by Liam Lawrence, took advantage of some weak refereeing. When Serran went missing in the 65th minute, Halford rose to head home the winner. It was unusual for the Swans to concede two goals at home and doubtless lessons were learned about how to deal with tough-tackling, hard-bitten professionals.

Once more, however, Swansea rallied strongly in the next fixture. Only 153 intrepid fans made the long trek to Portman Road for the Ipswich game on 4 December. Statisticians faithfully recorded the fact that the Swans enjoyed 70 per cent of the possession and that there were no off-side decisions throughout the entire game. What the home manager, Roy Keane, made of this is unknown, but it is a fair assumption that sharp words were said, as well as teacups thrown, after the final whistle. Having fallen behind on 50 minutes, Swansea began to turn possession into goals. Two splendid efforts by the energetic Beattie – a header and a right-foot drive into the top corner – and a toe-poke by

Allen brought three points, though the Swans were heavily indebted to de Vries, who made several fine saves, and to the marshalling powers of Ashley Williams.

The ebb and flow of results continued the following Friday when Swansea once again showed an aversion to playing under floodlights at night. Millwall were the visitors and their manager Kenny Jackett, who had successfully stamped his personality and methods on to his club, had a point to prove. On the night, physicality very nearly triumphed. The flustered hosts were forced into an alarming array of basic errors, misplaced passes and squandered chances. Although a header by Rangel set them on their way in the 18th minute, a goalmouth scramble rather like a scene from the Keystone Cops led to a deserved equalizer for the Lions. But for some woeful finishing and marvellous saves by de Vries, the visitors would have won the match in a keenly fought second half. Still, a point was a point and the Swans remained third in the league.

Yet there were difficult fixtures ahead, none more so than a trip on 18 December to the deafening cauldron at Bramall Lane where lowly Sheffield United, having just lost their young manager Gary Speed who had been appointed manager of Wales, were fighting to retain their Championship status. Swansea had not won there since 1939 and, although the team won the lion's share of possession, a lapse in concentration just before half-time allowed Ched Evans to break away and score the only goal of the game for the Blades. How costly would a defeat like this prove?

More woe was to follow on Boxing Day when the Swans were put to the test against league leaders Queens Park Rangers and found themselves outgunned in almost every position. Only Ashley Williams came out of the game with any credit. After falling behind in the 16th minute, the team's cause was hardly helped when the red mist descended on Alan Tate who was sent off following a scuffle with Clint Hill (who was also given a red card). With his customary positive approach Rodgers instructed his players to attack furiously, but this meant that the gifted Adel Taarabt, the best player in the division, was given greater room to display his creative, goal-scoring skills to devastating effect. A 0–4 defeat was a chastening result as the pressure of sustaining form in the promotion dog fight began to play on nerves.

Within two days, however, the team showed against Barnsley that even if bodies were tired, the spirit was still willing. Rodgers rang the changes and the recalled Dobbie was a revelation as the Swans returned to their winning ways. His first touch was excellent and his intelligent switching of play brought the best out of Dyer and Cotterill on the flanks. To the delight of the home crowd, Swansea threw caution to the wind, stormed forward at every opportunity, and were rewarded when Welsh international Jermaine Easter, on loan from MK Dons, swept home what proved to be the winning goal after 28 minutes. Stunning saves by de Vries in the second half proved vital as Barnsley pushed hard for an equalizer.

By the end of the calendar year, Swansea had played 24 league games and won half of them. With 40 points on the board, they stood in third place, just behind Cardiff on goal difference and just above rivals Leeds and Norwich. Their adventurous, attacking approach had not only borne fruit but had also won many plaudits. Players always like to command the respect of their peers, and the slick passing style of the Swans had won them many admirers within the game. In Brendan Rodgers they had a manager who inspired affection as well as respect, and there was every reason to suppose that the Swans could make his first season truly memorable. The dream of achieving promotion was still very much alive as 2011 beckoned.

4

The Push for Promotion

Wɪᴛʜ 22 ʟᴇᴀɢᴜᴇ games still to play in just over four months, much would now depend on the coming and going of players, the effects of injuries, and the galvanizing support of the Jack Army. Swansea were still in the FA Cup, but defeat at home to Leyton Orient in late January got rid of that distraction and, at least in hindsight, proved to be a blessing in disguise. Unlike much richer clubs in the Football League, Swansea had no Russian tycoons, Malaysian businessmen or Saudi sheiks to bankroll them and bring expensive young stars on loan to the club. But spirits were raised when striker Luke Moore, a young man with a good deal to prove, was signed from West Bromwich Albion on a two-and-a-half-year contract. Rodgers also shrewdly brought back the diminutive midfielder Leon Britton from the wilderness of Sheffield, a move which not only delighted the fans but would also prove crucial during the run-in. Less happily, Garry Monk sustained a serious knee injury early in January while playing against Colchester in the FA Cup and, at that late stage, it proved difficult to find a suitable replacement at centre-back. As ever, the versatile Tate was drafted in to shore up the centre of the defence. But concerns about Swansea's puzzling form against lowly opponents persisted as the fight against relegation at the bottom of the division threatened to leave its mark on the race for promotion.

None the less, the Swans started well in a hard-fought contest at Reading on New Year's Day. Darren Pratley, who had angered fans by refusing to commit his future to the club, silenced his critics by scoring a 65th-minute winner with a net-bursting volley from twelve yards. But the key to achieving the double over the Royals were three vital saves by de Vries. As games came thick and fast, however, defensive lapses took on greater significance. On 3 January, two embarrassing errors, both from corner kicks after 6 and 43 minutes, nullified a wonderful goal by Sinclair and cost the club three points at rapidly improving Leicester.

But fleeting doubts about the ability of the

team to sustain a promotion challenge were brushed aside on the following Saturday when a defensively minded Crystal Palace were disposed of with the minimum of fuss. The Swans dominated midfield, Dyer was at his irrepressible best and the Londoners duly wilted under the constant pressure. A sweet volley by the increasingly influential Pratley and two coolly taken penalties by Sinclair brought three richly deserved points. A week later Sinclair was calmness personified once more in dispatching a late penalty to claim a valuable, if hardly deserved, point at Barnsley.

Then, with one distressing exception, came a highly productive spell in February. Five wins propelled the Swans into second place by St David's Day, fuelling hopes of winning automatic promotion. Similar surges had of course occurred in the days of Martinez and Sousa, but a spirit of optimism was unquestionably in the air at the Liberty Stadium. Brendan Rodgers continued to vaunt the collective strength of the team and supporters hoped and prayed that fatigue and injury would not take their toll during the crucial last months.

Following the shock defeat at home against Bristol City earlier in the season, Swansea were determined not to allow them the opportunity to achieve a derby-double on a foggy night at Ashton Gate on 2 February. A goal in each half by Pratley sealed a convincing performance which delighted the 1,630 travelling supporters and put them in good heart for the south Wales derby scheduled for the following Sunday. As usual, this occasion received almost obsessive coverage in the Welsh media and 18,200 spectators packed into the Liberty Stadium for another lunch-time kick-off determined by the presence of Sky Sports cameras. Despite the cold weather, the atmosphere was electrifying. Both teams were by now extremely strong candidates for promotion. Cardiff were second in the table, Swansea third. With a glut of expensive on-loan players in their side, Cardiff were a much stronger outfit than had been the case in the first encounter and on this occasion Dave Jones got his tactics right. On the day, Cardiff were the better team. First to the ball, they pressed Swansea tirelessly, won most battles in midfield (where Joe Allen had been surprisingly left out of the starting line-up), and created the better chances. A piece of magic by Craig Bellamy decided the tie in the 85th minute. Receiving a pass from Aaron Ramsey at the edge of the box, he curled the ball exquisitely beyond de Vries's despairing dive. Luck was on Bellamy's side as the ball cannoned in off the post, but it was a goal worthy of winning any derby and capped a keenly fought encounter, notable for its nervous tension rather than its high-quality football. Bragging rights had returned to the capital and Cardiff's hopes of gaining automatic promotion had received a huge boost.

A lesser side might have wilted following this reversal and on finding themselves 1–3 down at Middlesbrough on the following Saturday. But what local reporters liked to call their 'bouncebackability' came to their rescue at the Riverside. Jittery in defence and slack in midfield, they had conceded three preventable goals before tactical changes helped to launch a dramatic revival. Goals by Dyer, Williams and Sinclair restored parity and an improbable left-footed scorcher by Beattie in the 94th minute brought victory against all the odds. Another high-octane performance at home against a Doncaster team ravaged by injury and illness led to a 3–0 win. Sinclair chalked up his nineteenth goal of the season, but the loudest cheers were reserved for the hard-working Moore, whose 78th minute goal was his first for the Swans.

A mid-week game at the Ricoh Arena in

Coventry in mid-February would not figure prominently on a professional footballer's wish-list unless he had a particular taste for a rugged, backs-to-the-wall performance against a tough, grizzly side. But Swansea were ready to compete and to hang on. The back-four were uncompromising, Dyer was a menace whenever he got the ball, and Rodgers's attacking instincts were rewarded when, five minutes after replacing Pratley, Stephen Dobbie hooked a bouncing ball over his shoulder into the top corner of the net. Once more, teamwork, spirit and tactical shrewdness had brought victory.

On the last Saturday in February, over 19,000 spectators, including nearly 3,000 visiting fans of Leeds United, most of them wearing their garish yellow away shirts, turned up at the Liberty Stadium to witness an absolutely riveting attacking performance by the home team. The first goal after 13 minutes was arguably the goal of the season. De Vries's pinpoint clearance to Taylor allowed him to cut inside before finding Sinclair who skipped into the box and played a cute one–two with Moore before stroking the ball past Kasper Schmeichel in the Leeds goal. On the other flank Dyer mercilessly tormented George McCartney, the Leeds left-back and a Northern Ireland international, and was such a constant threat that when he was bundled over by Gradel after 55 minutes referee Dowd had no hesitation in pointing to the spot. Sinclair faultlessly converted the penalty kick and a nicely worked third goal by the unsung Moore rounded off a complete performance. Crestfallen Leeds supporters were reduced to chanting 'We're not famous any more' and the blow to their pride was as great as to their chances of gaining promotion. By this stage, Swansea were back in second place as Cardiff began to falter.

The euphoria of February, alas, was replaced by anguish in early March when the Swans could only muster a point in three games, two of which were away fixtures against lowly opposition. Glanford Park is a joyless venue at the best of times and relegation candidates Scunthorpe made it even more uninviting by sanding their wretched pitch and getting stuck in to the apprehensive visitors. Amassing six yellow cards to Swansea's none simply spurred them on. Excellent chances that fell to Sinclair, Allen and Dyer were spurned, and when an inexperienced referee awarded Scunthorpe a controversial penalty after 71 minutes the home team pocketed three undeserved points. The dent to Swansea's morale was palpable and critics wondered whether the team had sufficient mental strength to win promotion. The same question was asked after a tepid 1–1 mid-week draw at home against Watford and even more loudly when the Swans wilted under strong physical pressure in a 1–2 defeat at lowly Derby. Even the normally reliable Ashley Williams was harassed into driving an intended back pass to de Vries into his own net. Did the team have the steeliness to match its talent? Rodgers certainly thought so and expressed his total confidence in his players.

To freshen things up, however, he persuaded Chelsea to allow him to borrow Fabio Borini, a promising young Italian striker whom he had mentored at Stamford Bridge and who arrived in time for the visit of rivals Nottingham Forest on 19 March. It was a perfectly timed move. Borini stamped his presence on the game, showing strength, mobility and goal-scoring prowess. After Sinclair had scored a wonderful goal on 21 minutes, beating four men during a mazy, high-stepping run into the box, Borini also chipped in with two opportunist goals in a 3–2 victory. Forest were outplayed and returned home feeling sorry for themselves. Swansea were cock-a-hoop and Borini's skill and youthful enthusiasm had restored a sense of optimism.

John Toshack always used to say that April was the key month in any season. For Swansea, it opened badly. Once more they were laid low by relegation strugglers, this time Preston, whose manager Phil Brown instructed his ground staff to disrupt the visitors' fluency by neglecting to cut the grass and his players to hustle their opponents into errors. Conceding a penalty after three minutes did not help Swansea's cause and, although Ashley Williams equalized with a header, the visitors faltered with just seven minutes left when Ian Hume was allowed to run virtually unhindered into the box and score convincingly. Swansea were now in fourth place with 66 points. Only one goal separated them from Cardiff.

On 9 April second-placed Norwich, buoyed by 2,000 supporters, arrived for an evening kick-off. Even though the game was to be televised, it attracted the largest crowd of the season to date. A total of 19,904 paying customers witnessed a rip-roaring performance by the Swans. Norwich were swept away. A superb free-kick from 25 metres by Borini, a technical masterpiece modelled on Didier Drogba's specialities, set the standard after five minutes. Then, completely out of the blue, goal-shy Mark Gower stole the scene. When the ball fell into his path on the edge of the box after 29 minutes, he hit an absolute purler which whistled past goalkeeper Reddy into the bottom corner of the net. It was his first goal for eighteen months and his celebrations were understandably loud and prolonged. A late goal by Tamas Priskin, a Hungarian international on loan from Ipswich, sealed a victory which brought the Swans to within two points of automatic promotion.

Then came two tricky fixtures against teams who were still in the hunt for the play-offs. Hull City arrived at the Liberty Stadium with a hugely impressive away record. Unsurprisingly, they came away with a share of the spoils even though Gower, now in rich goal-scoring vein, doubled his tally for the season for the home team with another superb goal. Then, on 16 April, defeat against Burnley at Turf Moor realistically killed off hopes of automatic promotion. Borini put Swansea ahead with his fourth goal in five games, but an own goal by Ashley Williams and a soft penalty decision robbed Swansea of the points.

Brendan Rodgers's motivational powers and tactical shrewdness were now put to the test. There were four fixtures left and he was determined to finish the season in the highest possible position, preferably above Cardiff. Conceding goals had become a problem and gritty defiance was expected of his players against Portsmouth at Fratton Park on 23 April. In his pre-match talk, Rodgers spoke of the 'warrior spirit' required in order to end the run of four consecutive away defeats. His players were left in no doubt that this was no time for faint hearts. In hot sunshine, the Swans put up dour resistance against Portsmouth, whose team of bruisers committed seventeen fouls in a bid to blunt the visitors' creative edge. Both sides managed only a shot apiece on target and the Swans were happy to come away with a goalless draw. In some ways it was the most valuable point of the season.

After this energy-sapping battle Swansea faced a resurgent Ipswich, now managed by Paul Jewell, on the Bank Holiday Monday. But there was no need to fret. The Swans overwhelmed the Tractor Boys, thanks to a brace by Borini, a goal by Moore and a penalty by Sinclair. All over the field Swansea were full of running, sharp and vibrant in setting up attacks, and deadly in front of goal. The 4–1 result was hardly a true reflection of their superiority. The Ipswich players had been given a master class.

Having secured a play-off place, Swansea

travelled to the Den in good heart even though they had not registered a win there for 81 years. Eight coaches of fearless supporters were given a police escort from Blackheath onwards and sang their hearts out in their eyrie in the away compound. Since Millwall still harboured hopes of reaching the play-offs and Swansea were aiming to finish the season in third place, a good deal was riding on this fixture. An additional item of interest was the growing possibility that the leaders Queens Park Rangers might be docked up to fifteen points for allegedly breaking the rules on third-party ownership, using unlicensed agents in signing Alejandro Faurlin, a talented midfielder from Argentina, and bringing the game into disrepute. To the great delight of the 958 Swansea supporters who ventured into Millwall's notoriously volatile ground, their team dominated the game from start to finish. Solid in defence and swift on the break, they coped admirably with every effort by their opponents to test their skill and temperament. Splendid goals, one in each half, by Pratley and Dobbie were no more than Swansea deserved and the Millwall staff, gracious in defeat, warmly praised what they described as the finest team-performance seen at the Den over the season.

Just one game remained: a home fixture on 7 May against Sheffield United, who had already suffered the indignity of being relegated and whose manager Micky Adams (who had once held the reins at Swansea for 13 days) blooded several youngsters in their line-up. Half an hour before the lunch-time kick-off news was received that, although Queens Park Rangers had been fined for their transgressions, no points would be deducted from their tally. This surprising outcome provoked a good deal of spiky comment as the players warmed up and Huw Jenkins later hinted that an appeal against the decision was not out of the question. The game was a notable one for Lee Lucas, the Aberdare-born midfielder and Wales Under-21 international, who came on as a second-half substitute and displayed touches which impressed both his manager and the home supporters. Visiting fans, wearing fancy dress, showed some gallows humour by dancing the Conga up and down the terraces behind the goal, but on the field Swansea showed their team no pity. The crowd of 17,584 were treated to a superb attacking display which brought four goals without reply. Two excellent goals by Dobbie – one of them a rasping free-kick from out wide – and a penalty by Sinclair sealed the victory, but the loudest cheers were heard in the 90th minute when Leon Britton, hardly the most prolific scorer of goals, produced a left-footed daisy-cutter to die for. The home team won 71 per cent of possession and made 757 passes, 92 per cent of which were successful. How delightful it was for the supporters to enjoy a stress-free afternoon in the sunshine and to be able to revive the old song 'Swans, Swans will tear you apart again'.

This was Swansea's 24th victory in the Championship, an achievement matched only by the winners Queens Park Rangers. Over the course of the season the Swans had scored 69 league goals, 29 more than in the previous season, and had kept 22 clean sheets. Their overall total of 80 points, together with a superior goal difference, assured them of third place, just above Cardiff. This was the club's highest position in the Football League since the 1981–2 season. Their opponents in the play-off semi-final over two legs would be Nottingham Forest, while Cardiff would face Reading. The South Wales Police heaved a sigh of relief on receiving this news and fans were soon forming orderly queues at the ticket office at the Liberty Stadium in readiness for two epic struggles against Billy Davies's men.

Before preparations began for the play-offs there was time to honour the most outstanding performances of the season at the club's annual awards dinner. Goalkeeper Dorus de Vries received the Players' Player of the Year and the Away Player of the Year awards, Nathan Dyer received the much-coveted Supporters' Player of the Year award, and Scott Sinclair was the unanimous winner of the Top Goalscorer of the Year award as well as the Goal of the Season award for his remarkable goal against Nottingham Forest in March. Welsh international defenders at the club made off with two other prestigious honours. Neil Taylor received the Young Player of the Year award and Ashley Williams's tireless charitable work earned him the Club Ambassador of the Year award. It was pleasing, too, to learn that Ashley Williams and Scott Sinclair had been included in the PFA Championship Team of the Year. The Supporters Trust also stimulated interest in the history of the club by setting up the Robbie James Hall of Fame, to which ten pivotal players would be inducted each year, and their achievements commemorated at the Liberty Stadium.

Yet it was the quality of the play and the squad's collective achievement which stayed in the mind once the 46 league games had been completed. In full cry, the team which Brendan Rodgers had coached and managed had been a splendid sight, controlling matches by controlling possession, scoring memorable goals and fully deserving its reputation as 'the Arsenal of the Championship'. It was not uncommon for some commentators to make comparisons with leading clubs in La Liga. Indeed, some jokers claimed that supporters of Barcelona at the Camp Nou would often gasp at the quality of their team's *tiki-taka* and say 'It's just like watching Swansea City!' As the club's match analyses reveal, over the season Swansea's pass count was a highly impressive 526 per game, a total far in excess of its Championship rivals. The average possession was an astonishing 61 per cent and the pass-completion rate a staggering 83 per cent. There was no better place to watch the 'beautiful game' than the Liberty Stadium.

5

The Play-off Semi-finals

I N A CURIOUS way, as the countdown to the first leg began, the pressure was on Nottingham Forest. Billy Davies, their fiery Glaswegian manager, who was still smarting after his team's play-off failure against Blackpool a year earlier, maintained that the time was ripe for his side to 'come of age'. Unlike his excitable counterpart, however, Brendan Rodgers was his usual unruffled self as a baying crowd of 27,881 supporters, including 1,700 Jacks, raised the temperature at the City Ground on Thursday evening, 12 May. Rodgers chose the same side as that which had demolished Sheffield United, meaning that his captain Garry Monk was on the bench. His ability to foster self-belief and a winning mentality was about to be put to the test. Could the Swans reproduce the courage and doggedness that had stood them in such good stead at Fratton Park and the Den? The

Swans had not won at Forest for five years and the hosts were in a rich vein of form, having recorded four successive wins in the final run-in. The man in the middle was Mike Dean, a fastidious referee who had done the Welsh team few favours in the past. It promised to be a night of remarkable drama.

The start could hardly have been more calamitous for Swansea. After just 53 seconds referee Dean, heavily influenced by the antics of the Forest manager and his staff, brandished a red card following a reckless rather than a malicious tackle by Neil Taylor on Lewis McGugan. Rodgers was forced to reorganize quickly. Dobbie was sacrificed for Monk and Tate filled in at left-back. Undeterred, the Swans pursued their game-plan, settling into their normal routine of passing the ball swiftly and accurately. For the rest of the first half, eleven-man Forest found themselves chasing shadows. Borini kept the Forest defenders fully occupied with his strong, incisive runs and sharp shooting. On three occasions, only the brilliance of Lee Camp in goal prevented him from giving Swansea a comfortable lead at the break. The home team's best chance came in the 37th minute when a fierce volley by Robert Earnshaw was superbly saved by Dorus de

Vries. Forest supporters could not but admire the ease with which the depleted Swans retained possession and how they showed that football at its best is about pace, skill and fluidity. Against all expectations, it was scoreless at half-time.

Forest were a different proposition in the second half. Throwing caution to the wind, they attacked incessantly. There were deafening shouts for a penalty when a goal-bound shot by Cohen struck Tate on the arm, but the referee remained unmoved. From the resulting corner Boyd flicked the ball on to Earnshaw whose header into the net from close range was correctly ruled offside by the assistant referee. Wise owls among the Swansea fans exchanged glances as they remembered that Earnshaw, like Filippo Inzaghi of AC Milan, had been born offside. Billy Davies fumed and fretted as his team lacked the wit to make their numerical advantage count. Swansea were magnificent and even after Borini left the field with a suspected hamstring strain their brave resistance continued. Monk and Williams were twin towers of strength in defence, Allen and Britton were as tireless as ever, and Dyer's willingness to run with the ball gave his hard-pressed colleagues a breather when needed. Indeed, with a little more composure, Dyer might have scored an unexpected winner a minute from time. At no time during the season was the Jack Army prouder of its heroes and, with the tie still goalless, the whole of Swansea now looked forward to an equally memorable second leg on Monday evening, 16 May.

In fact, the second leg turned out to be the most pulsating match ever seen at the Liberty Stadium. As the teams lined up, the physical disparity between the teams was striking. Billy Davies had made four changes in the hope that height and power would overwhelm Swansea's back-four and force de Vries to kick the ball long rather than short. From the outset Forest hoofed the ball forward with little regard for the memory of their former manager Brian Clough, who had always insisted that grass was God's most precious gift to footballers. From the first whistle Swansea's little men – Allen and Britton – remained at the hub of things, constantly showing for the ball and using it intelligently. Tate, who replaced the suspended Taylor, offered another outlet for his goalkeeper by venturing further up the left flank. Dyer was at his mischievous best and nearly drew first blood with fierce shots which were blocked by the towering centre-back Wes Morgan. Then Tyson broke away down the right and from his cross

McGoldrick clipped the bar with a rising shot. Back came Swansea. A humdinger by Borini was deflected on to the bar by Morgan, with goalkeeper Camp helpless. As the near-misses and surprises mounted, the crowd became increasingly vocal. While Brendan Rodgers remained calm, his counterpart fidgeted, moaned and cussed as his team struggled to gain ascendancy in this full-blooded encounter. One excited television commentator shouted mid-way through the first half: 'A sensational atmosphere here, real blow-the-roof-off stuff.'

Decibel levels soared even higher on 28 minutes. Following a well-worked short corner, the ball fell to Britton who turned a bemused Tudgay inside out before curling a glorious left-footed shot past Camp. Five minutes later Dobbie played a lovely one-two with Dyer, nutmegged Chambers and drove a low left-foot shot into the bottom corner of the net. Forest were reeling and were glad to hear the half-time whistle.

In the second half Forest pushed up twenty metres, but still lacked width as well as invention. Moreover, they spurned clear-cut chances. On 50 minutes Tudgay missed a sitter, blazing over from close range following a cross by Tyson.

Eight minutes later, much to the delight of those home supporters who believed that he had made a meal of Taylor's foul in the first leg, McGugan struck the bar from a free kick. As the pressure on Swansea grew, Rodgers replaced Dobbie with Pratley who, two minutes later, steered a free header wide when it looked easier to score. With greater composure, Borini might have added a third goal as Forest left gaps at the back in their search for a goal. No one could take their eyes off the pitch and throughout Britain armchair viewers remained glued to their television sets or computers. One blogger wrote: 'I followed the game online ... Well, I almost burnt my noodles! Breathtaking!'

Then, as experienced observers knew he would, substitute Robert Earnshaw decided to do his best to spoil the party. With ten minutes left, Rangel gave the ball away and Earnshaw pounced on a slide-rule pass from Majewski before beating de Vries emphatically at his near post. It was his first touch. In the 90th minute the little striker was millimetres away from scoring an equalizer when his shot struck the foot of the post and rebounded to safety. Even in added time Earnshaw was still determined to be the scourge of Swansea. Finding space in the six-yard box he hit a fierce cross which struck

Ashley Williams on the arm. The Forest players and their supporters howled for a penalty, but referee Andre Marriner waved away their protests as he awarded a corner.

Then came a frantic finale worthy of any episode of 'Roy of the Rovers'. As Forest prepared for the corner in the dying moments, their goalkeeper Camp sprinted forward to accompany the other giants in the box and add a bit of nuisance value. Was there to be one more surprise? Could anyone bear not to watch? In came the corner, de Vries punched it clear, McGugan miskicked and the ball fell to Pratley, whom most people knew was set to join Bolton in the close season. He set off for the halfway line, pursued by defenders and a despairing Camp. Britton screamed at him to make for the corner flag in order to waste precious seconds. But Pratley had only one thought in mind. He glanced up to get his bearings before reaching the halfway line on the right-hand side of the field. Then, from fully 55 metres and with consummate skill, he lofted the ball towards the vacant Forest goal. Hordes of Swansea supporters behind the goal then played their part by gleefully sucking the ball safely into the net. In wild celebration or perhaps in a gesture of farewell to the home fans, Pratley stripped off his shirt and dashed for the far touchline under the West Stand. Not to be outdone, Brendan Rodgers embarked on a spontaneous Mourinho-like sprint (only faster) along the near touchline of the West Stand, followed by his startled, puffing substitutes, before exchanging high fives with delirious spectators and basking in the glory of success. Pratley was booked for revealing his torso, but no one, least of all the player himself, cared. The final whistle sounded soon afterwards and Swansea had triumphed 3–1 on aggregate.

Never had the Liberty Stadium echoed to such an ovation, and the jubilant scenes will live long in the memory. Wembley beckoned and, once Cardiff had fluffed their lines in the other play-off tie twenty-four hours later, only Reading stood between Swansea and promotion to the top flight. An emotional Brendan Rodgers spoke of his pride in his players and supporters: 'They've got hearts the size of bin lids. And our 20,000 fans sounded like 50,000. What a night!'

6

The Wembley
Play-off Final

I T JUST SO happened that potentially the most
valuable match in the history of Swansea
City Football Club coincided with the 25th
anniversary of the play-off system. Over the years
a succession of thrilling and often controversial
spectacles had kept the season alive for rival
clubs, had brought in the crowds and filled
the coffers of the clubs involved, especially the
winners. Like most successful films and soap
operas, both the semi-finals and finals had
supplied more than their share of suspense,
joy and anguish. Just about everyone agreed
that they offered a fitting climax to a long and
arduous promotion campaign.

Swansea had been to Wembley before. In
1994 its supporters had travelled to one of the
world's most famous venues to win the Autoglass

Windshields Trophy by beating Neil Warnock's tough and uncompromising Huddersfield after a nail-biting penalty shoot-out. Three years later, under Jan Molby's stewardship, they reached the Third Division play-off final, where they fell victim to poor refereeing and Northampton's good fortune. But these games were held in the old and rather dowdy Wembley, whose dilapidated Twin Towers had lost their sheen. On Monday, 30 May 2011, the Jack Army arrived at a spanking new stadium, built at a total cost of £737 million and opened in 2007. The Twin Towers had been demolished and the ground's most distinctive architectural feature was now the Wembley Arch, a towering steel arch with an impressive 317-metre span reckoned to be the longest single roof structure in the world. Once this new cathedral of football, which could house 90,000 people, hove into view, Swansea hearts missed a beat. Eight years earlier, the club had seemed destined for relegation from the Football League. Now the opportunity had come for this team, as proud representatives of the city, to win promotion to the top flight and pass into legend.

From mid-morning onwards hordes of Jacks poured out of coaches and cars and out of the heavily crowded Wembley Park tube station.

Welsh accents were everywhere and as the fans made their way, singing and chanting, to the stadium, some of them took part in good-natured kickabouts with Reading supporters. Even policemen on foot and on horseback smiled at the antics of these benign invaders. Those with only a few pennies left to rub together blanched at the exorbitant price of refreshments en route and yearned for the cheap and cheerful pies of the Vetch Field. Cheers rang out when local hero John Hartson, who had forsaken his commentating role with S4C for the day in order to be among hard-core Jacks, was spotted walking up Wembley Way with his family. Around 500 supporters from Den Haag, with whom Swansea has a special affinity, were there to add their voices to the general hubbub. Lovers of the British game, especially those who had lived through 'the Swinging Sixties', stopped to admire the very fine statue of Bobby Moore, a Golden Boy in the mould of Swansea's own idol, Ivor Allchurch. The chants grew louder as the many thousands of excited fans made their way up escalators to the array of bars, restaurants and catering outlets within the stadium. Wizened supporters who recalled the noxious latrines at the Vetch Field could hardly believe that even a stadium as lavish as Wembley could boast 2,618 toilets. Moreover, as they entered the stadium they were delighted to find that every single one of them had a fantastic, uninterrupted view of the play, as well as ample leg room. At each end there was a giant television screen and down below, inside the running track, was a lush expanse of turf worthy of the Liberty Stadium. The Barcelona players had evidently kept their promise to the likes of Rangel and Orlandi not to churn it up by adopting kick-and-rush tactics in beating Manchester United in the Champions League final 48 hours earlier.

Could Swansea seize the moment and become the first club from Wales to enter the charmed circle of Premier League clubs? In preparing for the contest, Brendan Rodgers had left no stone unturned. 'Preparation, preparation, preparation' was his mantra. He was thoroughly familiar with Reading's style of play, the threat they posed and their frailties. Reading had been a Premier League team in 2006–8, had several international players in their defence, and sported devastatingly swift, goal-scoring forwards, notably Shane Long, who had scored 25 goals during the season. But he knew, too, that their full-backs were not spring chickens and that his own team had not only boundless talent but also the belief, patience and calmness required to carry the day. The players had every faith in him and his staff. As Ashley Williams put it: 'The man is ultra-professional. He demands 100 per cent every day, and he gives that himself.' Having completed the double over Reading during the season, Swansea were marginal favourites in the betting stakes, but such trifles never count on football's biggest stage.

The support for both sides was deafeningly loud. In all, 86,581 spectators were present and throughout their careers none of the Swansea players had performed before such a mighty and noisy throng. The pre-match razzmatazz was tailor-made for Kevin Johns, the club's chaplain and pitch announcer. His contribution as a thespian, a pantomime dame, an entertainer and a broadcaster, let alone his tireless charitable work, had made him a popular hero in Swansea. Whipping up enthusiasm was his forte and his cry 'This is our day!' produced a cheer which shook the stadium to its foundations. Fireworks exploded on the halfway line as the two teams, one in white and the other in blue, emerged from the tunnel, shook hands and lined up for the fray. Sporting a white rose on the lapel of his smart grey suit, Brendan Rodgers took his place in the technical area opposite his great friend and adversary Brian McDermott.

A nerve-shredding 90 minutes lay ahead as referee Phil Dowd blew the first whistle. Swansea shocked their fans by making a hesitant start. The more determined Reading carried the fight to them and dominated the first 15 minutes. Within 90 seconds Swansea could have fallen behind when a comedy of errors in the box forced a flustered Ashley Williams to boot the ball out of play. Goalkeeper de Vries was uncharacteristically jittery as Reading piled on the pressure. Jimmy Kebe, a startling blur of energy on the right wing, threatened to overwhelm Tate, while on the other flank Jobi McAnuff was full of guile and pace. In midfield the Royals disrupted Swansea's stylish passing rhythm and when full-back Griffin scythed Sinclair down after seven minutes, a foul which earned him the first booking of the afternoon, it was obvious that Reading were determined to retain the initiative both in terms of possession and psychology. Ruffled by their opponents, Swansea gave the ball away too often and looked especially vulnerable at corners. But Reading failed to make their early incursions tell. Allen and Britton began to string passes together and the team responded as strains of 'Hymns and

Arias' wafted down to the playing arena. Borini, who had fluffed an early free-kick, showed some spirit by obstructing goalkeeper Adam Federici and irritating the big Georgia international Zurab Khizanishvili, only to be booked by Dowd for his pains. At least this minor fracas showed that the Swans were not prepared to lie down.

Then, on 19 minutes, Alan Tate played a wonderful cross-field ball into Nathan Dyer's path just inside the penalty box. The tricky winger flashed past the lumbering Khizanishvili, but was clumsily brought down as he prepared to shoot. Referee Dowd was perfectly placed to award the penalty and up stepped Scott Sinclair. There is more than a touch of glamour about Sinclair, but in these circumstances it was his coolness which caught the eye. As the Reading players harangued the referee and Federici played the clown, he waited for the dust to settle and the crowd to fall silent before placing the ball on the spot and following the routine which had worked so well for him in the past. Arms akimbo, he waited for the whistle. Then he began his five-step run, coupled with a late feint. As Federici dived to his left, Sinclair rolled the ball calmly into the bottom right-hand corner of the net. A cool penalty by a cool dude. The roar from the Swansea end was deafening.

The din had hardly died down when Stephen Dobbie, who had tasted success with Blackpool in the play-off final against Cardiff in 2010, decided that the time was ripe for him to display some Scottish flair. He latched on to a pass by Rangel, turned past the out-of-sorts Khizanishvili, and outpaced the ageing Ian Harte down the right flank before squaring the ball. Federici got his hand to the cross, but the ball fell kindly for Sinclair who steadied himself before slipping the ball inside the post. The Swansea roar echoed around the ground once more. Crestfallen Reading fans sat in disbelieving silence. In just three minutes the scales had tipped strongly in Swansea's favour.

Reading worked hard to recover from these setbacks and to establish some momentum. After 29 minutes they came very close to reducing the arrears. A near-post header from a corner by the persistent Noel Hunt was a warning which Swansea failed to heed after the interval. Speed merchant Kebe continued to find acres of space on the right wing, though he often flattered to deceive. More often than not his runs came to nothing and Tate blocked many of his crosses or shots. His counterpart Dyer was much more incisive and after 40 minutes he sprinted gloriously past McAnuff down the right flank and into the box. His cross ricocheted off the hapless Khizanishvili into the path of the on-running Dobbie. Most players would have taken two touches, but the supremely confident Scot immediately lashed it into the far corner of the net with the sweetest of volleys. The goal was a technical masterpiece. Much to the delight of their rapturous followers, it stretched Swansea's advantage to three. Surely the game was over.

Back came Reading on the stroke of half-time. De Vries hesitated when he should have come to clutch or fist away a tantalizing cross by Karacan. Fortunately, the ball squirted past an equally hesitant Shane Long and a golden opportunity had been spurned. In added time Leigertwood stung de Vries's palms with a powerful drive, but the Swans managed to survive with their goal intact until the break. Before the game no one would have believed that the score-line at half-time would read Swansea City 3 Reading 0. But in the bars and cafés in the stadium the mood of the Swansea fans was strangely subdued and those who predicted a further avalanche of goals by their team were openly mocked. Anyone familiar with the history of play-off finals or indeed the history of Swansea City knew that the tie was far from over. Would their favourites weather the coming storm?

Whatever Brian McDermott said to his players during the interval – and he must have stressed the crucial importance of scoring first – he clearly managed to raise their spirits. Reading dominated the first 20 minutes of the second half as they had done in the first. The Swansea goal was placed under constant siege as their speedy opponents won corner after corner. In the 49th minute Hunt lost his marker Borini in meeting a corner by McAnuff and his near-post header ricocheted off Joe Allen's shoulder into the net. A frantic period followed. Swansea were driven back by remorseless attacks. A bad tackle by Allen earned him a booking and the team struggled to regain its former poise and cohesion. Rodgers resisted the temptation to stiffen midfield and his instinct was nearly rewarded when Dobbie went on a splendid run which took him within shooting distance. At the crucial moment, however, he scuffed his shot. Pratley replaced him and the Swansea fans, knowing that this was his swansong, hoped and prayed that he could calm things down.

But the pace of the game quickened as Reading rampaged forward. In the 57th minute the mercurial Kebe won another corner as his diagonal run into the box was foiled by Tate's sliding block. McAnuff took the corner, de Vries stayed stubbornly on his line, and Matthew Mills rose above Monk to power a header into the top corner. The Swansea fans sat in stunned silence. Opposite them jubilant Reading fans scented blood. Two minutes later, with the Swansea rearguard in disarray, a rasping shot by Karacan was deflected on to the post by Ashley Williams and, not to be outdone, Monk made a heroic lunge to block to Hunt's goal-bound shot when the ball fell into his path. Swansea gathered strength from these timely interventions and held their nerve. After 75 minutes Mark Gower replaced the limping Britton, who had made a huge contribution in midfield, and set about restoring a greater sense of cohesion. But as both teams tired, unforced errors crept in. Reading's physical presence at corners was taking its toll and the pressure, both mental and physical, was mounting. It was clear that whoever scored next would establish an irresistible momentum.

Inevitably, perhaps, the one Swansea player who took the initiative was a survivor of the vital game against Hull City in 2003. In those days of flighty youth Alan Tate could sometimes be an accident waiting to happen, but by now he had an older and wiser head on him. He had already set up the move which led to his team's first goal and he was raring to make the game safe. In the 79th minute he surged forward down the left and slipped a beautifully weighted pass through to Borini. The young Italian's pace was too much for Griffin who unceremoniously toppled him in the box. Once more referee Dowd was well placed to spot the offence and award the penalty. This time there were no protests from Reading as the luckless Griffin sat on the turf with his head in his hands. The Swansea fans watched with bated breath as Sinclair confidently stepped up for his second penalty attempt. This time Federici guessed correctly by diving to his right, but Sinclair not only struck the penalty harder but also lifted it above the goalkeeper's despairing outstretched arms. Swansea had regained the initiative just as the comforting west Walian rain they had left behind reached Wembley.

There were still moments of alarm during the last ten minutes as Reading launched a late rally. Two clearing headers by the diminutive Allen helped to relieve the pressure and when he was replaced by Luke Moore shortly before the end he was given a huge ovation by the appreciative Swansea contingent. Four minutes of added time seemed to last forever, but then Dowd's final blast of the whistle signalled the end of a heart-stoppingly exciting game. Swansea's supporters, many of whom had kicked every ball, fell into each other's arms in relief. Some were seen kissing strangers and others were weeping with joy. The players celebrated on the field by hugging each other and repeatedly tossing their manager into the air. Poignantly, too, they donned shirts bearing the name and picture of their former colleague Besian Idrijaz. Then their proud captain Garry Monk, who had played through pain in this and several other matches, led them up 107 energy-sapping steps to receive and lift the 2011 play-off trophy. 'Our supporters were incredible,' said a jubilant Brendan Rodgers, 'and it's nice to repay their faith and get promotion.' Until his or her dying day, those who witnessed this pulsating game will be able to say, with justifiable pride, 'I was there.' Swansea had become the first Welsh team to reach the Premier League. Fame and fortune now lay ahead of a club which had faced oblivion not so long ago.

The result offered food for thought for statisticians. In May 2003 Swansea had needed to win the last game of the season against Hull to stay in the Football League. Its captain that day was one Roberto Martinez and among his colleagues were Alan Tate and Leon Britton.

The hero of the day was James Thomas who, like Scott Sinclair, converted two penalties in scoring a hat-trick, and the game ended in a 4–2 victory. Who says that history never repeats itself?

There were heady celebrations both in London and Swansea that night. Never had the city been prouder of its team. Swansea is a community club, keenly aware of its roots, and it was only right and proper that it should make arrangements for everyone in the city to share its pride in the players' achievement by joining them in a public celebration the following evening. On 31 May an open-air double-decker bus, carrying the players and members of the staff, including Cyril the Swan, inched its way slowly from the Vetch Field to a civic reception hosted by the Lord Mayor at the Guildhall. All along the route, an estimated 30,000 people savoured the moment, especially when Brendan Rodgers began chanting, to a huge roar, 'We are Premier League, we are Premier League'. Bliss was it on that sunny evening to be a Swansea fan.

Appropriately, Brendan Rodgers kept a sense of proportion amid the celebrations by reminding ecstatic supporters that there were good and perhaps more important causes to support. In June, in the company of several prominent managers and former footballers, he successfully climbed Mount Kilimanjaro in aid of the Marie Curie Cancer Care charity. On his return he learned that his first opponents in the Premier League would be Manchester City, who were being bankrolled by the untold wealth of Sheikh Mansour bin Zayed Al Nahyan, at their palatial new home, the Etihad Stadium. The irony did not escape him.

Although the marvellous achievements of the manager and his players throughout the season, and the thrilling result at Wembley, etched themselves on our minds and memories, the image which lingers longest is the sheer joy on the faces of the Swansea supporters as they celebrated victory both within the stadium and during the open-air parade afterwards. The Jack Army is not a passive force. It draws its strength from the community and the club, and its spirit is enriched by success on the field. Long may it enjoy life in the Premiership.